CW00501946

Narcissism And Leadership

Brittany Forrester

Published by vincenzo nappi, 2021.

NARCISSISM AND LEADERSHIP

First edition. August 16, 2021.

ISBN: 979-8201441425

Written by Brittany Forrester.

Also by Brittany Forrester

Adult Survivors of Childhood Sexual Abuse The Effects On Mental Health And The Role Of Cognitive Behavior Therapy
Binge Killer The Use of Cognitive Behavioral Therapy to Address Shame in Binge Eating Disorder
Codependency Recovery Learn To Recognize Codependent Traits And Overcome Them
A Guide for the Psychosocial Treatment of Infertility
Emdr Toolbox A Powerful StrategyOf Self Through Eye Movement Desensitization and Reprocessing Therapy
Emotional Sugar Understanding Sugar Addiction, Through the Lens of Emotional Regulation
Face Failure Characteristics of Leaders Who Have Successfully Recovered from Significant Setbacks
Narcissism And Leadership
Childhood Experiences of Sibling Abuse An Investigation into Learned Helplessness
End Panic Attacks And Stop Anxiety
Self-Regulation Skills How To Control And Regulate The Learning Process
The Self-Esteem Workbook The multiple forms of self-esteem and the evaluation of one's value
The Shame Complex A Depth Psychological Exploration of Shame
Brain Healing and Trauma How Dark Psychology is Highly Effective in Treating Adult Survivors of Childhood Abuse

Complex Ptsd Recovery Understanding and treating Complex Trauma Using Emdr and Concepts from Individual Psychology
Defiant Children When Your Kid isn't Just Difficult
The Ultimate Diabetes Cookbook Take Control of your Type 2 Diabetes with a Complete Meal plan and Tons of Delicious Recipes
A Complete Guide to Parent Attachment How to Help Children to Heal From Trauma and Learn the Skills They Need for Successful Relationships

Table of Contents

Narcissism And Leadership

By

Brittany Forrester

Chapter 1 – General Introduction

Thomas Carlyle, one of the most acclaimed thinkers of the Victorian era and chief instigator of the "Great Man" Theory, believed that the destiny of humankind as a species fell on the shoulders of great men, who were intelligent, charismatic, influential and powerful. In doing so, Carlyle could have possibly prophesied at that time the subsequent rampant "culture of narcissism" that we observe in modern society – a society in which everyone wants to be great. Today, more people than ever are paying more attention to writing their "autobiographies" of greatness, even when the content is not all that "great". Often within these potentially rather narcissistic autobiographies, there exists a common chapter on leadership and how it is a viable path towards "greatness". However, whether narcissists actually achieve greatness through leadership is less straightforward - due to the dynamic interaction between narcissism, leadership and the social world, and the changes this interaction undergoes as a function of time. Thus, the aim of the current book is to unravel the changes in narcissistic leadership that develop over time and to examine the potential mechanisms that are responsible for any such changes. This introduction will address the temporality of narcissistic leadership by first presenting a broad overview of the relevant narcissism and leadership literature, followed by an appraisal of the temporal relationship between narcissism and leadership. Next, the introduction will cover the mechanisms that might explain the temporality of narcissistic leadership, namely, transformational leadership and evolutionary strategies of gaining social status.

Narcissism

The term "Narcissism" is derived from Ovid's tale of Narcissus falling in love with his own reflection to the detriment of his true/real self, which caused him to perish. Although Ovid's tale of Narcissus being obsessed by his image is void of any psychological examination, it is significant not merely for where the term "narcissism" is derived from, but more importantly for the constructive themes (e.g., unrequited self-love) that resonated with later interpretations of narcissism as a personality trait. The early moulding of narcissism as a personality trait was perhaps most notable in the field of psychoanalysis, where narcissism was initially theorized as a universal process within normal psycho-sexual human development (Freud, 1905/1957), but was subsequently developed as a self-regulatory personality process, more specifically as a module of self-preservation (Freud, 1914/1957; Rank, 1914/1971). According to Freud (1914/1957) this module of self-preservation operates dynamically by consistently obscuring information and feelings that would diminish the sense of self. Both Freud and Rank believed that this self-preservation is achieved through exhibiting grandiosity as a defense against vulnerability of the self. A narcissistic individual engaged in self-preservation would demonstrate high independence, extraversion, low likelihood of being intimidated, aggression and aversions to love or close relationships (Freud, 1931/1959; Levy, Ellison, & Reynoso, 2011). Freud found that these characteristics combined to create "personalities" that impress, can be relied upon and can readily assume leadership positions, especially when radical shifts from the status quo are sought after by would-be followers. Further, the extent to which narcissists are willing to construct their grandiose selves for the purposes of self-preservation seems to be boundless. For instance, Kohut (1985) likened Freud's construction of the narcissistic self to an admired omnipotent model:

"Certain types of narcissistically fixated persons (even bordering on the paranoid)...display an apparently unshakeable self-confidence and voice their opinions with absolute certainty...Such individuals' maintenance of their self-esteem depends on the incessant use of certain mental functions...they are continually judging others – usually pointing up the moral flaws in other people's personality and behaviour – and, without shame or hesitation, they set themselves up as the guides and leaders and gods of those who are in need of guidance, of leadership, and as a target for their reverence."

These psychoanalytical perspectives suggest that narcissists regulate their self-image through portrayals of grandiosity, which are often boundless, in turn leading to their rise into leadership positions.

Sculpting Narcissus: Self-regulation to construct and to maintain self-concept

The pioneering work in psychoanalysis has contributed significantly to the current understandings of narcissism as a personality construct. Indeed, contemporary definitions of narcissism include reference to relevant psychoanalytic concepts, particularly narcissists' motivation towards self-preservation that is achieved through grandiose displays. Narcissists are described as individuals who possess inflated, overly-positive and predominantly agentic self-views, who pervasively employ self-regulatory strategies in order to maintain or enhance this self-views, and who have interpersonal relationships that lack empathy and emotional intimacy. This definition captures various aspects of personality, resulting in narcissism being situated at the "nexus of personality", where examinations of the self, self-regulation, and relationships are interconnected and can be approached concurrently.

The Dynamic Self-Regulatory Processing Model and The Extended Agency Model are two prominent self-regulatory models that have admirably integrated all the bridging elements of narcissism to explain the dynamic nature of the construct. Although both models possess components and theorizing that distinguishes one from the other, a key similarity between them is their focus on self-regulatory processes.

Narcissists engage in these self-regulatory processes to maintain or enhance their grandiose self-views, through intrapersonal (or intrapsychic) and interpersonal strategies. Intrapersonal strategies employed by narcissists include fantasizing about personal achievement, heroism, power, and self-adulation, displaying overconfidence even in the face of failure, distorting, disregarding or being overly-defensive of negative feedback and self-handicapping. Interpersonal self-regulatory strategies include showing off and dominating conversations, amassing and flaunting material goods, performing better when others are watching, having a preference for famous partners and asserting their power to gain leadership in leaderless groups.

Although the definition of narcissism seems to focus on agentic self-enhancement as the predominant aim in narcissistic self-regulation, the engagement in the various intrapersonal and interpersonal self-regulatory strategies is context-dependent. More precisely, the employment of self-regulatory strategies is dependent on the appraisal of whether a specific context affords narcissists opportunities for self-enhancement or if threats to positive self-construction are present.

Engaging in self-regulation that is context contingent suggests that narcissists might be more attracted and better suited to temporal contexts that they construe as self-enhancing, relative to temporal contexts that are either not self-enhancing or present threats to narcissists' positive self-construction.

Sculpting Narcissus: The two faces of narcissism

Narcissists' ability to appraise situations as an opportunity – threat appraisal, and their subsequent engagement in self-regulatory strategies is likely a consequence of narcissistic grandiosity juxtaposed with fragility of the self. Similarly, work examining narcissism within broader personality models such as the Big Five, Interpersonal Circumplex and Five-Factor Model has also demonstrated a narcissistic personality construct comprising grandiose and vulnerable characteristics. For instance, narcissistic grandiosity is characterized by extraversion and disagreeableness, whereas narcissistic vulnerability is characterized by neuroticism and disagreeableness.

It is evident in the literature that narcissism as a personality construct comprises two distinct dimensions: narcissistic grandiosity and narcissistic vulnerability. However, the degree to which these two dimensions of narcissism operate independently of each other or conjointly remains unclear. Thus, we have made it a point to consider and measure both narcissistic grandiosity and narcissistic vulnerability in this book. Nonetheless, the findings to date seem to imply that narcissistic grandiosity is the dominant facet of narcissism in the context of leadership. As such, we placed a greater focus on examining the relationship between narcissistic grandiosity and leadership in this book.

Leadership

In a meta-analysis of the personality-leadership literature, Judge et al. (2002) sought to clear up any confusion that could arise from the muddling of leadership outcomes by distinguishing between leader emergence and leader effectiveness. Leader emergence refers to being perceived as leader-like, as an individual's quantity and quality of participation in a group, or the influence exercised and social status attained in a group. One common characteristic across all the definitions of leader emergence is that it is based heavily on perceptions, usually those of observers or peers. Contrastingly, leader effectiveness refers to a leader's performance in influencing and guiding the activities of his/her unit towards the achievement of its goals. Ratings of leader effectiveness can be derived from followers and superiors, which, however, are only modestly correlated. This weak correlation alludes to the variation in leader perceptions between superior and follower, thereby emphasizing the uniqueness of follower perceptions of leader effectiveness relative to superior perceptions. Thus, greater consistency in leadership findings can be attributed to the creation of clearer conceptual boundaries of leader emergence and effectiveness alongside greater use of follower perceptions, to measure more accurately leadership effectiveness.

Leadership temporality

Besides being two conceptually different aspects of leadership, leader emergence and leader effectiveness also occur at distinct temporal phases, with leader emergence preceding leader effectiveness. As mentioned earlier, a major criticism of the individual-centric approach to leadership research has been the neglect of considering the various environmental influences while examining leadership outcomes. Organizational environments can often be complex, and subject to uncertainty, discontinuity, and continuous change.

In order to account for the fluidity of environments where leadership takes place, it is important to recognize leadership as a dynamic process where multiple factors can culminate in the making or breaking of leadership. Conceptualizing leadership as a dynamic process has led leadership theorists to advocate explorations into the temporal effects of leadership, as well as the complex developments within self-regulatory and interpersonal processes.

Taking the relevant leadership literature into consideration, we subscribe to the views that

1) leader emergence and leader effectiveness are two conceptually distinct leadership outcomes that feature in temporally distinct phases;

2) follower perceptions offer a more accurate reflection of leader emergence and leader effectiveness and;

3) leadership is a dynamic process that centers on relationships between leaders and followers that could be heavily influenced by time.

The demise of narcissus: Narcissistic leadership and its durability

The Chocolate Cake Model was initially developed to explain the dynamic processes responsible for the temporality of romantic relationships with narcissists, which was typified by initial positive perceptions that waned over time. In order to explain how certain narcissistic traits are (mal)adaptive across different situations and contexts, the chocolate cake model was extended to develop the more contextually encompassing the Contextual Reinforcement Model. Based on a costs and benefits framework, the Contextual Reinforcement Model proposes that narcissistic traits are likely to be adaptive in contexts that are classified as "emerging" zones and maladaptive in the "enduring" zones. This context-dependent approach is also consistent with psychodynamic models of narcissism, where narcissistic self-appraisal and subsequent self-regulatory processes are sensitive to contextual changes. Whether or not a context is considered emerging or enduring is determined by the extent to which self-enhancement is possible. Narcissists would be attracted to and strive to gain entry to contexts that are construed as self-enhancing, and abstain from or exit contexts that are not. Contextual or temporal changes to self-enhancement opportunities cause a "natural" drift from emerging to enduring zones, which implies that due to changes in the social context, adaptive outcomes derived from the initial demonstration of narcissistic traits alone are destined to be short-lived. When applied in the context of narcissistic leadership, it is likely that narcissists would be perceived positively as leaders initially but that these positive perceptions would wane over time.

Observed perceptions of narcissists also seem to support the honeymoon nature of narcissistic leadership, where there is an emphasis on making positive first impressions rather than preserving existing relations. For instance, narcissists are high in extraversion and possess confidence and strong social skills, which are essential for effective social interaction in leadership. The initial attractiveness of narcissists for leadership positions extends well beyond extraversion. Indeed, narcissists are also known to make better first impressions, which likely contribute to their tendency to emerge as leaders, particularly in zero-acquaintance situations. Further, their attraction to power has also been shown to bring about follower perceptions of narcissists as emergent leaders, beyond the effects of extraversion. However, with increasing acquaintance, narcissists are more arrogant, are less entertaining, tend to brag and overestimate their abilities. Thus, theorization on narcissistic leadership and perceptions of narcissists seem to suggest that the temporal pattern of narcissistic leadership is characterized by a short honeymoon period that rapidly wanes.

Explanatory mechanisms of the temporality of narcissistic leadership

Owing to the dynamic natures of both narcissism and leadership, narcissistic leadership can only be facilitated when the evolvement of narcissism and its consequent leadership behaviors are aligned with the dynamic social processes that characterize different temporal phases of leadership. From a narcissist's perspective, demonstrating appropriate leader behaviors at appropriate temporal leadership phases is only a secondary consideration if any, because their self-regulation only engages in self-enhancement and not purposefully in leadership per se. Thus, mechanisms that explain the temporality of narcissistic leadership would need to demonstrate that narcissists engage in self-enhancing behaviors that are perceived positively initially for leadership but not overtime. One potential mechanism that might demonstrate an evolvement of such narcissistic leadership behaviors across time is transformational leadership.

Transformational leadership

Transformational leadership is an approach to leadership that involves establishing relationships with followers through personal, emotional, and inspirational exchanges so that followers are motivated to perform beyond their expectations. Transformational leadership is closely related to charismatic leadership, given the latter's similar focus on establishing emotional and inspirational exchanges with followers through visionary aspects of leadership. Consequently, followers are able to internalize these emotional and inspirational exchanges as part of their self-esteem, resulting in greater commitment to and willingness to achieve their goals. The similarity between transformational leadership and charismatic leadership is also evident in the literature, where these two leadership concepts have been recognized as being synonymous. However, while similarities do seem apparent, some have argued that charismatic leadership alone cannot possibly account for all forms of personal, emotional and inspirational exchanges between leader and follower. So instead of recognizing the interchangeability between transformational leadership and charismatic leadership, charismatic leadership is considered a component of transformational leadership, mainly by capturing the visionary and/or inspirational aspects of charismatic leadership. Although charismatic aspects are integral to the conceptualization of transformational leadership, the notion that transformational leadership comprises components beyond charismatic leadership elements has provided added gumption for a more multifaceted approach. Consequently, a slew of other compatible transformational leadership qualities has been created: idealized influence, appropriate role-modeling, fostering acceptance of group goals, high-performance expectations, intellectual stimulation and individual consideration, which can be further simplified into vision, support and challenge components. Transformational leadership is also considered an effective form of leadership and has been associated with a myriad of positive outcomes, including leader effectiveness, leader and/or group performance, satisfaction with the leader, follower motivation, and job satisfaction.

In the context of narcissistic leadership, whether narcissistic behaviors are perceived as transformational, and in turn as effective leaders could account for why narcissists are favored at specific temporal phases and not others. This explanatory utility of transformational leadership at the temporal level is evident in the equivocal findings in the narcissism-transformational leadership literature. For instance, US Presidents who were classified as more narcissistic were considered more charismatic. Similarly, transformational leadership has been found to be positively related to narcissism. Contrastingly, narcissists have been deemed as less transformational leaders. These equivocal findings suggest that it is possible that narcissistic leadership explained through transformational leadership could be susceptible to temporal effects. More precisely, there might be certain temporal phases where narcissistic traits are recognized as transformational and other temporal phases where they are not.

Chapter 2 - Evolutionary basis of leadership, narcissism, and narcissistic leadership

Other potential explanations for the temporality of narcissistic leadership can perhaps be unearthed if we consider narcissistic leadership within the broader conceptual framework of evolutionary psychology. Examining narcissistic leadership within an evolutionary framework seems a natural step to take given that there already exists theorizing on the evolutionary origins of both narcissism and leadership.

Evolutionary theories of leadership

The main premise of evolution is to succeed in the competition to survive and to reproduce (i.e., evolutionary fitness), which can be achieved through selected adaptations that maximize fitness benefits and minimize fitness costs. These selected adaptations have evolved to address chronic and recurrent problems that affect the chances of survival and reproduction. Psychologically evolved adaptations in leader-follower relationships are no different, as they are likely to have evolved over time to provide solutions to group coordination problems. Specifically, group coordination requires group decisions on a myriad of problems to maximize survival chances, which could be facilitated by the emergence of a leader – which in turn suggests that leadership is selected as a positive adaptation that enhances evolutionary fitness.

Although leadership arises as a consequence of group coordination problems, which suggests leadership as a provider of group-level fitness benefits, evolutionary perspectives of leadership propose that it is also possible to consider fitness benefits at the individual level, thereby generating further insights on the evolution of leadership. Integral to the individual level inquiry of the evolution of leadership is the view that leadership involves interactive cooperation between leader and follower that is governed by the principle of "reciprocal altruism". Reciprocal altruism refers to the mutually beneficial exchange of fitness costs and benefits between leader and follower, in that a potential leader would only find it worthwhile to incur fitness costs and provide fitness benefits to others when fitness benefits can also be reciprocated to them for their initial act of "altruism". Altruistic reciprocity shares parallel with transformational leadership as they both focus on the interaction between leader and follower. However, a key difference between these two approaches is that while transformational leadership is able to provide proximal explanations for leadership, altruistic reciprocity affords a more historic view of why we are (un)attracted to certain leaders.

As mentioned earlier, evolutionary perspectives of leadership deem leadership as a solution to group coordination problems and an individual who is prepared to incur fitness costs to benefit others is likely to be considered as the leader. However, according to the principle of reciprocal altruism, a mutually beneficial leader-follower relationship only materializes when followers compensate leaders for the fitness costs they have incurred to benefit them. In such instances, followers compensate leaders by conferring them with social status. Social status is a valuable currency in the leader-follower exchange of fitness costs and benefits and can be attained by engaging in either prestige or dominance strategies. Prestige refers to the attainment of higher social status through the achievement of expertise that is valued and respected by others without the need for coercion. Contrastingly, dominance refers to the attainment of social status through the use of intimidation and coercion, mainly through the induction of fear. Although prestige and dominance are conceptually distinct from each other, both have been shown to be viable pathways to achieving leadership.

However, an understanding of which social status strategies are involved in influencing leadership over time seems elusive.

In order to identify the salience of social status gaining strategies on leadership over time, it is crucial to consider the unique contextual characteristics that define each temporal phase of leadership. Service-for-Prestige Theory could offer some insight into the reasons why leaders might engage in one strategy over the other - by predicting the evolutionary systems that typify each temporal phase of leadership. For instance, service-for-prestige theory contends that leaders are especially likely to provide public goods during initial group formation, where group coordination is urgent. Since there is empirical evidence to suggest that both prestige and dominance are distinct, yet equally viable strategies for achieving leader characteristics of high social rank and influence, individuals who can provide solutions towards group coordination, either through prestige or dominance strategies, would likely be recognized by group members as emergent leaders. However, beyond leader emergence, the public nature of the leader's contribution would most likely result in a collective action problem where leaders incur fitness costs to provide public goods (i.e., contributions that benefit all group members), while followers, incentivized by a higher net fitness benefit, receive public goods and decide to free-ride by not conferring (sufficient) social status to the leader. Unless mechanisms such as punishment and social exclusion are in place to neutralize the advantages of free-riding, leaders might disengage from the leader-follower relationship by offering either fewer or no public goods. Persisting with a prestige strategy is bound to fail, as it does not curb free-riding behavior. Although dominant individuals tend not to be well-liked, engaging in a dominance strategy could be deemed necessary and acceptable even by followers, in order to facilitate leadership functions such as enforcing rules within the group to neutralize the advantages of free-riding, thereby minimizing the collective action problem. Thus, from a temporal perspective, prestige and dominance could independently and differentially determine leader effectiveness across time.

Evolutionary theories of narcissism

Although social status is valuable currency within the evolutionary leader-follower exchange of fitness costs and benefits, it is important to note that one's identification with social status seems to be mitigated by self-enhancement. Unsurprisingly, self-enhancement is also underpinned by evolutionary principles, where self-enhancing behavior is characterized by effective decision-making, attractive portrayal of mental and physical health, and gaining higher social status and/or leadership roles. The value of self-enhancement in achieving evolutionary fitness has instigated investments in psychological processes with evolutionary bases that can assist in self-enhancement; such as self- and other-deception, and overconfidence.

Coincidentally, self-regulatory models of narcissism also posit that narcissists arc heavily reliant on self-enhancement to regulate their inflated self-views with their genetic associations. Given narcissism's genetic intimations, it is unsurprising that there have been scholarly predictions on the evolution of narcissism.

The first evolutionary theory of narcissism emerged from a mating perspective, where an early preference for short-term mating is hypothesized to be responsible for the evolution of a variant of dominance – or narcissism. It is only about 1.5 million years ago that hominids, who originally focused on attractiveness and contentiousness (corresponding to promiscuity and short-term mating), also started to invest in cooperativeness (corresponding to long-term pair-bonding) as a reproductive strategy. The viability of short-term and long-term mating strategies among humans has resulted in an evolutionary state whereby elements of both attractiveness and contentiousness (giving rise to socially aversive narcissistic tendencies) and cooperativeness (complex self-concepts that are descriptive of narcissists) are positively selected for. However, for narcissists, their evolutionary preference for short-term mating has manifested into their propensity to engage in competitive behaviors, such as narcissists' inclination towards status-striving and clamor for leadership positions. In the case of the latter, relationships with narcissists also tend to take the form of initial positive impressions, which are usually fleeting, such as in a leadership context where narcissists are likely to succeed to emerge as leaders in newly-acquainted groups, but not overtime.

The second evolutionary theory of narcissism posits that narcissism has evolved to operate on a balance of implicit shame against hubristic pride. Stronger convictions in implicit shame ultimately pervade the temporary veil of hubristic pride, which limits narcissists to pursue only short-term successes. The emotion of pride is conceptualized as two distinct and independent facets: hubristic and authentic. Hubristic pride is characterized as arrogant and conceiting, while authentic pride is characterized by feelings of accomplishment and confidence. Although both facets of pride have been evidenced to evolve to enhance social status, hubristic pride, in particular, maybe an evolutionary adaptation to promote a dominant strategy of acquiring social status.

Thus, it is believed that narcissism, comprising early life experiences of implicit shame and other associated negative dispositional traits, could promote a dominance-oriented regulatory system that is programmed to seek status through the explicit demonstration of hubristic pride, which acts as a coping mechanism going into uncertain status-enhancing environments. Further, this emotional projection of hubristic pride to attain status is consistent with evolutionary notions of self-deception, where self-enhancement has evolved as a means for individuals to deceive themselves and others. Thus, from a narcissistic leadership perspective, narcissists' evolved effective system is likely to lead them to adopt dominance strategies to gain leadership. More specifically, adopting a dominance strategy that is fuelled by implicit shame and explicit displays of hubristic pride, allows narcissists to be psychologically better equipped than others to cope with the demands of uncertain group coordination situations such as leader emergence. Although both prestige and dominance are equally viable ways to attaining leadership, narcissists probably do not see the need to switch from a dominance approach to a prestige approach. However, with reference to the aforementioned literature on the evolution of leadership, narcissists' evolutionarily enforced persistence with dominance strategies is unlikely to make them effective leaders over time.

Taken together, these two evolutionary theories of narcissism suggest that narcissists are likely to have adapted largely dominance strategies for leadership. These dominance strategies preferred by narcissists also seem to tend towards short-term, immediate gains, which are reflective of their initial success during leader emergence, but not overtime.

Chapter 3 -The Leader Ship is Sinking: A Temporal Investigation of Narcissistic Leadership

Relationships with narcissistic leaders can be a paradoxical experience, much like eating chocolate cake. The first bite of a chocolate cake is usually rich in flavor and texture, and extremely gratifying. After a while, however, the richness of this flavor makes one feel increasingly nauseous. Being led by a narcissistcould be a similar experience: Narcissists might initially be perceived as effective leaders, but these positive perceptions may decrease over time. Originally developed to explain romantic relationships with narcissistic individuals, the Chocolate Cake Model has since been applied to describe the relationships between narcissistic leaders and their followers.

Although the chocolate cake model is applicable to the temporal effect of narcissistic leadership, this effect remains complex because of the dyadic and dynamic nature of leadership. Thus, understanding the dynamic and complex nature of the relationship between narcissism and leadership requires investigations that move beyond the simplistic position of examining whether narcissists make "good" or "bad" leaders. However, despite repeated calls, there is currently no direct test of the temporal relationship between narcissism and leadership in the literature and no theoretical consideration of the role of transformational leadership within that temporal relationship. We aim to test the temporal component of narcissistic leadership with a view to examining whether being led by people higher in narcissism is akin to eating chocolate cake. In providing the first empirical test of this theoretical position, we also present and explore a possible explanatory mechanism of this effect.

Narcissism and leadership

The notion that narcissists have traits that lead followers to perceive them as leaders have been well-documented in the literature. Self-regulatory models describe narcissists as individuals with positive, inflated, and predominantly agentic self-views who employ self-regulatory strategies in order to maintain or enhance this self-views. Thus, narcissists would be expected actively to seek out positions of leadership, because such positions might serve to promote their self-enhancement. From the perspective of the follower, narcissists seem to possess some of the requisite traits for effective leadership. For example, narcissists' extraverted disposition allows them to be socially skilled and appear likable. Beyond extraversion, narcissists are also charismatic, perform well in public tasks and difficult situations, and exude an aura of confidence and dominance. Furthermore, many illustrious positions of leadership (e.g., the US presidency) have been occupied by individuals rated higher in narcissism. In summary, individuals higher in narcissism seem to possess traits that predispose followers to perceive them as effective leaders.

Is narcissistic leadership durable?

Despite their possession of seemingly effective leadership characteristics, narcissists are often rated negatively on their leadership qualities.

One potential explanation for this paradox is the way that leadership has been conceptualized in the literature. That is, leadership has typically been defined and measured in two distinct ways: leadership *emergence* and leadership *effectiveness. Leadership emergence* is achieved by exercising influence or attaining high social status in a group of strangers. Contrastingly, *leadership effectiveness* is achieved by judgments of one's performance as a leader. Thus, leader emergence and leader effectiveness are conceptually distinct and occur at distinct temporal phases, with leader emergence preceding leadership effectiveness. Despite the vast potential influence of temporality on a multitude of leadership behaviors and outcomes, there is a surprising dearth of consideration and evidence for the importance of temporality in leadership research.

The issue of temporality (or lack thereof) is equally evident when considering narcissistic characteristics and leadership. Indeed, many of the traits that propel narcissists into positions of leadership have been posited to be the same as those that precipitate their eventual downfall. Narcissists at limited acquaintance might initially be perceived favorably as leaders because they are more extraverted. Individuals high in extraversion possess confidence and strong social skills, which are essential for effective social interaction in leadership. The initial attractiveness of narcissists for leadership positions extends well beyond extraversion, however. Indeed, narcissists are also known to make better first impressions, which likely contribute to their tendency to emerge as leaders, particularly during zero-acquaintance situations. Further, their attraction to power has also been shown to bring about follower perceptions of narcissists as emergent leaders, beyond the effects of extraversion. There is thus evidence that positive perceptions of narcissists in zero-acquaintance situations increase the likelihood of narcissists being regarded as emergent leaders. However, with increasing acquaintance, others view narcissists less favorably because narcissists are more arrogant, less entertaining, tend to brag, and overestimate their abilities. This temporal change highlights the importance and influence of acquaintance level on the temporal perceptions towards narcissistic leadership; whereby individuals higher in narcissism are deemed positively as leaders by newly-acquainted others, but less so by well-acquainted others. Consequently, since acquaintance is developed through accumulated interpersonal interactions over time, the variant findings between short- and long-term acquaintance suggest that temporality may be responsible for differences in perceptions of narcissistic leadership. As such, temporality of leadership is central to understanding the dynamics of the relationship between narcissism and leadership – an understanding that is currently plagued with inconsistency in the literature.

The nature of the narcissism-leadership relationship over time is compounded by the reciprocal influence that both the leader and the follower can have on the leader-follower relationship. Although self-regulatory models of narcissism have allowed researchers to understand leadership through the lens of a narcissist, these models fail to account for the perspective of the follower and the potential temporal impact on the leader-follower relationship. As such, it is important to consider theoretical models (e.g., chocolate cake model) that might complement such self-regulatory models by providing a focus on the perceptions of those who are engaged in relationships with narcissists. Such a consideration would allow us to understand how changing contexts over time might lead to different perceptions of narcissistic leaders.

Despite the theoretical advances that have been made regarding the dynamic relationship between narcissism and leadership, there is a dearth of evidence supporting this theorizing. The closest empirical evidence for the temporal nature of the narcissism-leadership relationship comes from research focusing on the social cost of narcissists' decision-making strategies. Campbell et al. demonstrated that narcissists' decision-making strategies focused on short-term gains at the expense of long-term benefits. Although these findings are somewhat supportive of narcissists' better performance in the short-term compared to the long-term, the decision-making paradigm does not integrate the social-interactional nature of leadership and thus cannot shed light on the temporal effectiveness of narcissistic leaders. It is this relative temporal effectiveness that is the focus of the present studies.

Transformational leadership as a mechanism

There is likely a complex interplay between narcissism and leadership across time, and the specific mechanism via which the temporality of this relationship might unfold remains unclear. One likely explanation is that the specific changes in narcissists' leader behaviors evolve over the course of leadership. Specifically, transformational leadership might explain why narcissistic individuals are perceived initially as leaders and why such positive perceptions might wane over time. Transformational leadership is an approach to leadership that involves establishing relationships with followers through personal, emotional and inspirational exchanges so that followers are motivated to perform beyond their expectations. Additionally, transformational leader behaviors are associated with a myriad of positive outcomes, including leader effectiveness, leader and/or group performance, satisfaction with the leader, follower motivation, and job satisfaction. Indeed, the charismatic and visionary components of transformational leadership, which are positively linked with narcissism, will likely result in narcissists being initially perceived as effective leaders. Thus, followers' perceptions of narcissistic leaders' effectiveness could be explained by narcissists' exhibition of transformational leadership behaviors.

The outcomes manifested through transformational leadership are also likely susceptible to the influence of time. For example, the positive impact of an inspirational speech given by a transformational leader might be short-lived unless its underlying vision is consistently reinforced by the leader's actions over time, and unless the leader expresses belief in the followers' ability to achieve that vision. Narcissists' ability to articulate a vision could influence followers to perceive them as transformational at the initial stage of leadership. However, given narcissists' continual striving for self-enhancement and personal glory to the extent of exploiting others for personal gain, their transformational leadership behaviors are likely to fade over time. Consequently, it is likely that transformational leadership will mediate the relationship between narcissism and leadership effectiveness early during leadership, but not later. Specifically, the temporal reduction in this mediating effect is likely to be attributable to narcissists' diminishing display of transformational behaviors rather than any change in the well-established relationship between transformational leadership and leader effectiveness.

Discussion

Individuals rated higher in narcissism were initially perceived as leaders, but these perceptions disappeared over time; this finding was as hypothesized and is consistent with the chocolate cake model. Transformational leadership significantly mediated the relationship between narcissism and leadership early on but this mediating effect also dissipated over time. This dissipation was largely a specific reflection of the dissipation of the narcissism transformational leadership relationship. Indeed, the effect of transformational leadership on leadership remained consistently positive across each of the four-time points. This finding is informative because it supports previous research that has revealed a strong association between transformational leadership behaviors and effective leadership and suggests that the leadership decline of individuals higher in narcissism is associated with a relative decline in the degree to which they display transformational leadership behaviors.

Beyond the initial stage of leadership, positive follower perceptions of narcissistic leadership could gradually be damaged by the perceived lack of transformational leadership behaviors on offer, as individuals higher in narcissism are more likely to display behaviors that serve their drive for self-enhancement. In the initial stage of leadership, however, it is likely that individuals higher in narcissism have the ability to portray visionary aspects of transformational leadership making them attractive as leaders. Indeed, followers find visionary leaders more appealing than representative leaders who focus on their group's collective identity. Besides *vision*, transformational leadership also comprises strong *support* and *challenge* components, both of which could be particularly crucial beyond the initial stage of leadership. For example, *individual consideration* is a *support* component of transformational leadership and narcissists' relative lack of individual consideration may well contribute to the eventual decay of their leadership effectiveness.

Individuals rated higher in narcissism might also be positively perceived as leaders during the initial stage of leadership by virtue of being placed in a context that is optimal for them to emerge as leaders.

Narcissists are attracted to leadership because it is perceived as an opportunity for self-enhancement. Evidently, an element of self-enhancement appears critical to motivate narcissists to act upon something. Drawing from previous research on task persistence, it seems that narcissists are more likely to persist in their leadership roles only to the degree that competing opportunities for self-enhancement are absent. Such persistence might be hard to enact in reality, however. Indeed, narcissists are less likely to delay gratification and more likely to take advantage of more immediate opportunities for self-enhancement over more complex self-enhancing opportunities. This fixation on instant self-enhancement suggests that narcissists can be effective leaders provided that they are constantly focused on short-term self-enhancing goals. Additionally, when working in groups, narcissists perform better as leaders by engaging in more non-verbal communication and team assistance under the context of high reward interdependence, which suggests that narcissists can be drawn towards self-enhancement through the achievement of group goals. Consequently, organizations can encourage narcissists to be more effective leaders over time by structuring more self-enhancing short-term leadership goals that are highly interdependent. For example, traditional annual work reviews can be restructured into regular monthly reviews where narcissists' leadership performance is judged by team feedback and performance.

Although the decline of initial positive peer perceptions of leadership appears characteristic of narcissistic leaders, a temporal pattern of leadership is rather more universal. Termed the "honeymoon effect", this temporal decline is thought to be caused by leadership stagnation that could emerge from overconfidence, homogeneity, or complacency. Narcissistic leaders might suffer from the honeymoon aftermath much like any leader displaying the aforementioned traits since leader training and selection criteria, in general, seem to promote narcissistic characteristics that are favorable towards leader emergence in the first place. Thus, an overemphasis on the qualities that promote leader emergence not only suits narcissists but could also lead to a higher concentration of narcissists in leadership positions, and paradoxically less effective leadership.

Chapter 3 –The Leader Ship is Destined to Sink: An Evolutionary Perspective on the Decline of the Narcissistic Leader

The origins of leadership probably occurred 2.5 million years ago, when ancestral humans, the genus *Homo*, roamed the earth. The concept of leadership adopted by the genus Homo was widely considered to resemble that of the Melanesian "Big Man", described as, "...like a banyan ... though the biggest and tallest in the forest is still a tree-like the rest. But, just because it exceeds all others, the banyan gives support to more lianas and creepers, provides more food for the birds, and gives better protection against sun and rain.".

"Big Man" leadership was dominant because leadership in characteristically egalitarian societies at that time was limited by the expertise and granted only by followers. However, in the present-day human societies have become increasingly hierarchical, rendering "Big Man" leadership unsuitable across various contemporary situations and contexts. In its place, researchers have begun to examine other prominent leadership traits that may help to explain leadership (in)effectiveness. Of relevance to the present study is the personality of narcissism.

The current popularity of narcissistic leadership is supported empirically. Given their drive for self-enhancement, it is not surprising that narcissists actively pursue and are highly successful in achieving leadership positions. However, positive peer perceptions of narcissistic leaders only last for a short honeymoon period, as narcissists are eventually rated negatively by their peers. The temporality of narcissistic leadership clearly indicates that narcissistic tendencies can either be adaptive or maladaptive for leadership, and the extent to which these tendencies are adaptive or maladaptive is largely dependent on time. From an evolutionary perspective, self-enhancement is considered an evolved self-disposition that can be satiated through the achievement of high social status by prestige and/or dominance strategies. Thus, narcissists' obsession with self-enhancement and their initial highly successful pursuit of leadership positions could be an evolved psychological adaptation in attempts to guarantee their *survival* over time. Consequently, placing the temporality of narcissistic leadership within an evolutionary framework could offer potential explanations for the temporally dynamic relationship between narcissism and leadership. In this study, we apply an evolutionary framework to examine the temporality of narcissistic leadership and to investigate the evolutionary strategies that could be responsible for the rise and fall of narcissistic leaders over time.

Evolutionary perspectives of leadership

Although a wealth of research exists within current psychological investigations on leadership, much of this literature has been disparate and little attempt has been made to integrate them under a unifying theoretical framework. Evolutionary theories have offered complementary explanations to psychological postulations and could possibly provide a suitable encompassing framework to integrate psychological empirical findings in leadership.

The main premise of evolution is to succeed in the competition to survive and reproduce (i.e., evolutionary fitness), which can be achieved through selected adaptations that maximize fitness benefits and minimize fitness costs. These selected adaptations have evolved to address chronic and recurrent problems that affect the chances of survival and reproduction. Psychologically evolved adaptations in leader-follower relationships are no different, as they are likely to have evolved over time to provide solutions to group coordination problems. Specifically, group coordination requires group decisions on a myriad of problems to maximize survival chances, which could be facilitated by the emergence of a leader – which in turn suggests that leadership is selected as a positive adaptation that enhances evolutionary fitness. However, psychological findings on leadership depict that not all people are attracted to – or suitable as – leaders. This view is consistent with evolutionary theorization that leadership and followership co-evolve in humans, which implies that these roles can be adaptive under the right conditions. Natural selection favored humans who had the ability to procure cultural information, by getting close to and learning from knowledgeable and/or skilled others in the group. In return for increased social learning, the fitness cost for followers would be for them to defer benefits (e.g., by offering food, mates, etc.) to these knowledgeable and/or skilled others, who in turn benefit from the deference and grant followers permission to copy their knowledge and skills. This "exchange" between copying knowledge and skills and providing deference in return is an elaborated form of "reciprocal altruism", which, when balanced, can lead to optimal leader-follower relationships.

The notion of reciprocity to create mutually beneficial leader-follower relationships is further extended by an evolutionary model, where two paths are proposed for attaining social status: *prestige* and *dominance.* Although prestige and dominance are conceptually distinct from each other, both have been shown to be viable pathways to achieving leadership. Prestige refers to the attainment of higher social status through the achievement of expertise that is valued and respected by others without the need for coercion. Contrastingly, dominance refers to the attainment of social status through the use of intimidation and coercion, mainly through the induction of fear. Thus, the leader-follower relationship is operationalized by an exchange of fitness costs and benefits that are achieved through the means of prestige and dominance.

The service-for-prestige theory suggests that besides private goods, leaders also provide public goods (e.g., assume fitness costs by coordinating group members to acquire a shared resource) and should be compensated by receiving prestige collectively from the group. The assertion that leaders provide public goods is perhaps most evident during initial group formation, where group coordination is urgent. Individuals who can provide solutions towards group coordination, either through prestige or dominance strategies, would likely be recognized by group members as emergent leaders. However, the public nature of the leader's contribution would most likely result in a collective action problem where leaders incur fitness costs to provide public goods (i.e., contributions that benefit all group members), while followers, incentivized by a higher net fitness benefit, receive public goods and decide to free-ride by not conferring (sufficient) prestige to the leader. Unless mechanisms such as punishment and social exclusion are in place to neutralize the advantages of free-riding, leaders might disengage from the leader-follower relationship by offering either fewer or no public goods. Although dominant individuals tend not to be well-liked, it might be necessary in order to either: a) facilitate leadership functions such as enforcing rules within the group to neutralize the advantages of free-riding, thereby minimising the collective action problem, or b) achieve a leadership position from which leaders are in the position to administer prestige strategies. This postulation furthers the current understanding that both prestige and dominance are distinct, yet equally viable strategies for achieving leader characteristics of high social rank and influence particularly from a temporal perspective, where prestige and dominance could independently and differentially determine leader effectiveness across time.

The temporality of narcissistic leadership within an evolutionary framework

As described earlier, self-regulatory motivations of narcissism and the evolutionary perspectives of self-enhancement have identified self-enhancement as key to the preservation of narcissistic self-views and the enhancement of human evolutionary fitness respectively. Thus, it is unsurprising that narcissists, in their evolutionary quest to survive and reproduce, are attracted to attaining leadership positions; and have developed evolved psychological adaptations to maximize their success in doing so. Consequently, viewing narcissistic leadership from an evolutionary social status perspective can not only offer insights into the evolutionary interplay between leadership and narcissism but also potentially explain the temporal changes in narcissistic leaders' downfall.

Narcissists tend to succeed as emergent leaders particularly in newly-acquainted groups, where leader-follower roles are not yet established. As we have alluded to earlier, the context of working together in newly-acquainted groups effectively presents a group coordination problem that requires leadership; and narcissists, who covet self-enhancement in the form of higher social status, take advantage of certain evolved narcissistic adaptations in order to emerge as leaders. Since leader-follower roles would have been uncertain during initial group formation, service-for-prestige posits that leaders and followers share mutual social bargaining power, and potential leaders are likely to establish reciprocity with potential followers by offering public goods in return for prestige. This is consistent with previous findings on how narcissistic leaders are often the preferred choice during situations of uncertainty, possibly with the understanding that during times of leadership uncertainty, adopting prestige strategies that aim to establish reciprocity would be best practice. However, the uncertainty of the leader emergence context also hinges on superficial and fickle leadership perceptions that could impact narcissists' chances on leader emergence. Consequently, employing dominance-oriented strategies such as exuding an aura of confidence could also help narcissists to cope psychologically with the uncertainty of establishing themselves as emergent leaders. Thus, both dominance and prestige strategies are effective strategies towards leader emergence, which is empirically supported by how both prestige and dominance are effective for achieving social rank and influence among newly-acquainted groups.

Beyond the period of leader emergence, positive follower perceptions of narcissistic leaders disappear over time; which has been attributed to the negative influences of narcissistic characteristics such as being exploitative and losing sight of group goals in their pursuit of self-enhancement. However, positive and significant correlational peer-ratings in existing athletic teams between narcissism and dominance and leadership and dominance seem to suggest that narcissistic leaders are likely to be positively perceived by followers beyond the period of leader emergence if they engage in a dominance strategy. These findings are consistent with the conditions post-leader emergence, where narcissists have achieved higher social status through leader emergence, and in turn greater social bargaining power. This greater social bargaining power might prompt narcissists to prefer a dominance strategy in order to maximize net fitness benefits, and they can do so without risking negative follower perceptions of them as leaders because a dominance strategy could be construed as attempts to enforce rules to stem followers' free-riding behavior. Contrastingly, continuing to adopt a prestige approach would not only prevent narcissists from capitalizing on the short-term self-enhancement gains they thrive on, but also increase the possibility for follower free-riding to occur. Furthermore, the presence of competition from the out-group creates an in-group bias that can further consolidate the legitimacy of adopting dominance over prestige strategies because leaders are seen as organizing their groups against external competition.

However, as narcissistic leaders persist with dominance strategies, followers suffering from chronic net fitness losses (by deferring but yet not receiving any benefits from the leader) would have an increased collective intent to reject narcissistic leaders, which consequently results in followers' positive perceptions of narcissistic leaders to disappear over time. Thus, narcissists adopting dominance strategies immediately after leader emergence would prolong positive follower perceptions of narcissistic leadership, but prolonged adoption of dominance would result eventually in the waning of followers' positive perceptions of narcissistic leadership.

Discussion

The purpose of the present research was to examine the mediating roles of prestige and dominance on the relationship between narcissism and leadership across time. This temporal investigation utilized a longitudinal experimental design with groups of minimally-acquainted members. We observed that narcissists were rated positively as leaders initially but not later on.

When the mediating effect of prestige was considered, we found that prestige mediated the relationship between narcissism and leadership initially, but not later on, as hypothesized. These findings are consistent with previous empirical results that prestige is a viable means to leader emergence. Additionally, it is noteworthy that a consistent, significant positive relationship between prestige and leadership was revealed across all time points. This consistent relationship empirically supports service-for-prestige, where followers are adapted to positively perceive leaders who demonstrate the willingness and ability to provide them with benefits. However, more pointedly in the context of narcissistic leadership, this consistent relationship suggests that follower perceptions of narcissists as leaders are primarily dependent on the extent to which narcissists are able to demonstrate prestigious leadership behaviors. The reason why narcissists were perceived as prestigious leaders initially could be because narcissists' confidence, charisma, and social skills enabled them to convince followers that narcissistic leaders have high levels of domain-relevant expertise. The authenticity of narcissists' high levels of domain expertise would be difficult for followers to ascertain in the beginning but not overtime, which explains why narcissistic leaders' initial prestigious impression is eroded across time.

When dominance was considered as a mediator, we found positive indirect effects of narcissism predicting leadership via dominance initially and after the initial phase of leader emergence, but not at the later time points. Additionally, the relationship between dominance and leadership approached significance at Time 1, which was significant at Time 2 and non-significant later on. This latter effect indicates that, narcissism notwithstanding, individuals employing a dominance approach would be positively perceived as leaders early on but not later. The temporal findings were largely as hypothesized and support the notion that dominance is a viable means to leader emergence. Dominance may also qualify as a crucial stabilizing force within groups in a tumultuous post-leader emergence environment that is represented by follower free-riding and out-group hostility. The long-term effect of dominance was as hypothesized and supports the notion that engaging solely on leader dominance on a prolonged basis is disadvantageous to followers.

The temporal changes in follower perceptions of narcissistic leadership can be explained by two service-for-prestige postulations. First, service-for-prestige predicts that dominant leadership would come to the fore when followers lack exit options. When followers lack exit options, their social bargaining power reduces, and this, in turn, encourages leaders to maximize net fitness benefits by disregarding follower interests. For followers, being in a group led by a narcissist early in the experiment would arguably be further away from "exiting" the group compared to the latter stages of the experiment when they are closer to "exiting". Thus, followers' positive perceptions of narcissistic leaders' dominant strategies early on but not later correspond to the proximity followers were from exiting the group. Second, followers prefer leaders who deliver ingroup advantage and this follower ingroup bias is intensified in the presence of outgroup hostility, also known as the "rally effect". The rally effect provides followers with security through a willingness to cooperate with the leader against external rivals, while leaders benefit from gaining status. Since the rally effect enhances leaders' status, the propensity for it to be abused for greater power is highly probable. In the current study, narcissistic leaders, being characteristically manipulative and exploitative, were likely to take advantage of the rally effect to consolidate their leadership in the early stages of the experiment. However, as the rankings of the groups became more apparent in the latter stages of the experiment, outgroup competition weakened, which in turn led to declines in the rally effect and any consequent efforts to maintain leadership.

Taken together, the results show that the application of an evolutionary framework does offer unique perspectives on the mechanisms with which narcissists are temporally viewed as leaders by their followers. The results in the current study are consistent with previous assertions that both prestige and dominance are viable ways to leadership attainment. However, the viability of prestige and dominance strategies on leadership across time was found to vary among narcissistic leaders. Specifically, beyond the period of leader emergence, the waning follower perceptions of narcissists as leaders are explained by narcissistic leaders' consistent lack of engagement in prestigious behaviors. The findings for dominance yielded more complex predictions of narcissistic leaders' utility of dominance strategies across time. First, dominance had a stabilizing effect that was crucial for optimal group functioning in the period after leader emergence. Second, narcissistic leaders engaged in a dominance strategy in order to harness its short-term usefulness towards leadership and disengaged from it eventually as engaging solely on dominance was no longer perceived by followers as a viable long-term leadership strategy.

Evolutionary theories of narcissism

Evidence of a genetic basis linked with narcissism supports notions of an evolutionary basis for narcissism. The first evolutionary theory of narcissism posits narcissism as an evolved variant of dominance, so it is in narcissists' being to prefer dominant strategies, and consequently short-term self-enhancement in leadership. This theory emerged from a mating perspective about 1.5 million years ago when hominids, apart from focusing on attractiveness and contentiousness (corresponds to promiscuity and short-term mating), also started to invest in cooperativeness (corresponds to long-term pair-bonding) as a reproductive strategy.

The viability of short-term and long-term mating strategies among humans has led to the emergence of narcissism as a variant product - where elements of both attractiveness and contentiousness (giving rise to socially aversive narcissistic tendencies) and cooperativeness (complex self-concepts that are descriptive of narcissists) are positively selected for.

This intertwined evolution of cooperative and attractive and contentious adaptations suggests that narcissists are often caught in predicaments that are reflected in paradoxical accounts of narcissists as leaders. For example, narcissists have been positively perceived as leaders as well as negatively perceived as leaders. From a temporal perspective of narcissistic leadership, the intertwining of long-term and short-term mating traits could explain why narcissists are willing to engage in groups in order to pursue self-enhancement despite being socially aversive; which is consistent with how narcissists are able to successfully emerge as leaders in newly-acquainted groups. Over time, short-term mating adaptations take over and narcissistic leaders adopting dominant strategies would eventually be perceived as ineffective. This lack of long-term narcissistic leader effectiveness under the current climate of intertwined cooperative and attractive and contentious adaptations, could to a certain extent mean the dilution in the effectiveness of short-term mating manifested narcissistic tendencies. Such a conjecture implies that narcissists are likely to further evolve to incorporate more cooperativeness into their repertoire of self-enhancement strategies, in order to thrive in social environments that place cooperativeness at their core. This evolution towards a more cooperative brand of narcissistic self-enhancement is evident in previous research on narcissistic self-enhancement adaptations in communal settings, as well as narcissists' adaptiveness in incorporating communal traits like perspective-taking, which could translate to long-term leadership effectiveness. However, for narcissistic leadership in its current evolutionary state, short-term mating processes seem to be the default strategy adopted - consequently leading to a preference for short-term self-enhancement.

The second evolutionary theory of narcissism posits that narcissism has evolved to operate on a balance of implicit shame against *hubristic pride*. Stronger convictions in implicit shame ultimately pervade the temporary veil of hubristic pride, which limits narcissists to pursue only short-term successes. The emotion of pride is conceptualized as two distinct and independent facets: *hubristic* and *authentic*. Hubristic pride is characterized as arrogant and conceiting, while authentic pride is characterized by feelings of accomplishment, confidence, and stress. Although both facets of pride have been evidenced to evolve to enhance social status, hubristic pride, in particular, has been selected to promote a dominant strategy of acquiring social status. Thus, it is believed that narcissism, comprising early life experiences of implicit shame and other associated negative dispositional traits, could promote a dominance-oriented regulatory system that is programmed to seek status through the explicit demonstration of hubristic pride, which acts as a coping mechanism going into uncertain status-enhancing environments.

Further, this emotional projection of hubristic pride to attain status is consistent with evolutionary notions of self-deception, where self-enhancement has evolved as a means for individuals to deceive themselves and others. From a narcissistic leadership perspective, narcissists are successful in leader emergence because a) they are social status hungry individuals fueled by implicit shame, and b) explicit displays of hubristic pride allow them to be psychologically more well-equipped than others to cope with the demands uncertain group coordination situations. However, the short-term utility of hubristic pride in achieving leadership also highlights the inadequacy of solely relying on hubristic pride to cope with persisting in leadership positions over the long-term. Given the conceptual and empirical links between hubristic pride and dominance, the eventual disengagement in dominance strategies by narcissistic leaders, coupled with the short-term utility of dominance on leadership reflected in the current study seem to reinforce the notion that hubristic pride and/or dominance in isolation is ineffective for positive long-term narcissistic leadership. Future research can examine if narcissists' preference for short-term self-enhancement opportunities is limited by the narrow utility of hubristic pride/dominance (i.e., as a coping mechanism reserved for uncertain social contexts like leader emergence).

Non-evolutionary perspectives

Although the aforementioned evolutionary theories of narcissism do successfully explain the temporal effects of narcissistic leadership, it should be noted that these effects are not exclusively explained by evolutionary theories alone. For instance, self-regulatory theories of narcissism could explain why narcissists are seen as prestigious initially but not overtime. More specifically, narcissists could engage in prestige strategies that are more impactful in the short-term, rather than other strategies that are less impactful in the short-term but more temporally resilient. For example, narcissists could invest more heavily in self-regulatory processes like boasting and name-dropping, which immediately implies perceptions of prestige that are more impactful in the short-term, over demonstrating competence in the task at hand, which takes more time to achieve perceptions of prestige. Narcissists' impulsivity towards self-enhancement and their focus on short-term self-enhancement seem to support such a postulation. Thus, future research could investigate if favorable initial perceptions of narcissists as prestigious leaders that wane over time are due to narcissists' preference for engaging in prestige strategies that are more impactful but only effective in the short-term.

Intrapersonal factors such as the manner in which narcissists express their self-superiority beliefs and how followers infer such behaviors could explain followers' shifting perceptions of narcissistic leaders' dominance. Self-superiority beliefs have been associated with diverse outcomes ranging from social rejection to social acceptance and this diversity of outcomes could be dependent on how self-superiority is expressed. The Hubris Hypothesis has been developed to demonstrate how one's self-superiority claims are expressed can determine how observers perceive the claimant's self-view, and how observers, in turn, infer liking for the claimant. More specifically, observers infer from explicit self-superiority claims that the claimant has a negative view of others, which the observers, in turn, infer as the claimant having a negative view of them. Finally, observer inferences that the claimant has a negative view of them lead observers to evaluate the claimant unfavorably. In the context of narcissistic leadership, perceptions of dominance strategies are favorably perceived initially because group members are likely to accept other in-group members self-enhancing to become more socially accepted, and only object to others' self-enhancement when they are at a cost to them. According to the hubris hypothesis, group members incur social costs when they begin to interpret a narcissistic leader's explicit dominance as claims that narcissistic leaders are better than them. However, why this interpretation of dominance that leads to others' dislike for narcissists occurs in a later temporal phase is questionable and is worthy of future research.

Environmental characteristics of human society

The modern societies have evolved from earlier egalitarian iterations and arrived at increasingly hierarchical ones. This evolutionary transformation of human society is evident in today's unprecedented levels of income inequality in the developed world. For example, CEO incomes in the United States between 2000-2013 are 200-400 times that of the average worker. Consequently, achieving higher social status through leadership has never been more important in today's society - where narcissism has possibly evolved to help humans become more adept at attaining self-enhancing leadership positions. Contrastingly, as shown in the current study, narcissistic leaders are clearly inept in keeping their followers positive about their leadership across time, due to their persistence in dominance and lack of investment in prestige strategies. Narcissistic leaders are probably cognizant of their inability to remain as effective leaders over time and one strategy is to look for other short-term self-enhancement opportunities. Another strategy that narcissistic leaders can employ, especially when competing opportunities for self-enhancement are scarce, is to persist with dominance to inflict fear and ultimately forcing the submission of their followers because increasing fear inevitably increases the cost of challenging superiors. Additionally, greater transitivity of deference (i.e., if A defers to B and B defers to C, then A defers to C) in dominance relative to prestige could also result in the superiors of narcissistic leaders overlooking negative follower perceptions of being dominated by narcissistic leaders. The reality that leaders in most organizations are no longer chosen or sanctioned by followers via a bottom-up approach, but by their superiors is a reflection of how a dominance approach can be useful for leadership, even beyond the short-term. The applied ramifications of such leader selection and/or vindication practices are reflected in managers' perceptions that pleasing superiors are more instrumental to career success than pleasing followers. Narcissists are well-positioned to benefit from these increasingly hierarchical, top-down societal structures because all that is required of them is to attain leadership positions, dominate their followers into submission and engage in strategies to please their superiors. Thus, this notion that narcissists are suited to modern hierarchical societies complements the aforementioned postulations that narcissism is an evolutionary psychological adaptation that enhances human survival and reproduction.

Narcissistic leadership does not last long

The previous theorizing has predicted that the relationship between the narcissistic leader and their followers is contingent on its temporality. From a narcissism perspective, the temporal effects of narcissistic leadership underscore the importance of conceptualizing narcissism as a dynamic self-regulatory process where the narcissistic self is constantly being updated and modified as a consequence of the changing factors that affect self-regulation and vice versa. From a leadership perspective, our findings demonstrated the complexity of leader-follower relationship processes with respect to time, which is in line with calls for temporally-based leadership research. Studying the temporality of narcissistic leadership allowed us to break down the complexities of narcissistic self-regulation, and the interactions with their construal systems and social environment, into definitive chunks that are characteristic of a particular temporal phase/context. The variation in perceptions towards narcissistic leadership across time offers an explanation for the equivocal results on narcissistic leadership that has been observed across cross-sectional studies – that differences in perceptions of narcissistic leaders are possibly due to temporal/contextual changes. Further, according to Implicit Leadership Theory, followers' perceptions of leadership tend to change with the situation, providing support for the argument that follower perceptions of narcissistic leaders change over time because of the changing context of leadership. Indeed, this view of temporally/contextually dependent narcissistic leader-follower relationships is consistent with previous findings that have demonstrated narcissistic leadership to be susceptible to contextual differences.

The initial favoring of narcissistic leaders that wanes over time possibly correspond with temporal changes in follower perceptions of narcissists' self-enhancement behavior. Self-enhancement operates primarily for the benefit of the self and in doing so, there might be trade-offs incurred as a consequence especially since self-enhancement is considered to be contextually/temporally influenced. Such a view seems to suggest that the temporality of narcissistic leadership is dependent on the self-enhancement behaviors of narcissistic leaders, and how followers perceive these self-enhancing behaviors across time. Indeed, the Contextual Reinforcement Model shows that narcissistic leaders undergo a "natural drift" from an initial "emerging zone" where self-enhancement is more cost beneficial to an "enduring zone" where self-enhancement involves more trade-offs (to both narcissistic leaders and their followers) to the extent that considering exit strategies could prove more advantageous to self- image preservation. The temporality of narcissistic leadership is a consequence of corresponding contextual/ temporal self-enhancement benefits and trade-offs, highlighting the importance of taking a temporal approach in narcissistic leadership as opposed to a snapshot approach. Thus, taking a temporal approach is crucial because it affords greater sensitivity towards the temporal changes in social and personality parameters that influence the social-cognitive and self-regulatory processes that define narcissistic leadership.

Narcissists' preference for short-term self-enhancement could be innate

Given narcissists' apparent preference for short-term self-enhancement, it seems that narcissists are "programmed" to be attracted to and coincidentally possess the requisite leadership behaviors to achieve short-term self-enhancement, and therefore are less likely to demonstrate leadership behaviors that are appropriate for the long-term.

It is possible that the process of narcissistic self-regulation is dictated by a "time-bomb" mechanism where the default self-enhancement strategy is focused on the short-term. The existence of such a mechanism suggests that narcissistic self-regulation is not merely contingent on opportunities for self-enhancement, but on self-enhancement that requires less time to achieve. Equally, it is possible that narcissists' higher success in the short-term is not because they are strategic about short-term self-enhancement, but simply because they are impulsive by nature. Impulsivity is the dispositional lack of self-control that is akin to ego under control, which could explain narcissists' inability to consistently meet the high self-regulatory demands that are required to preserve their inflated self-image – which is more evident when observed in the long-term.

Other conceptualizations of narcissism might also offer potential explanations for narcissists' preference for short-term self-enhancement. One mitigating factor of narcissists' preference for short-term self-enhancement could be their implicit vulnerability of the self. The insecurities associated with narcissistic vulnerability could be inhibiting the extent to which narcissistic self-enhancement is pursued over time. Indeed, narcissism has been proposed as a source of hardiness in the face of adversity, but only when self-esteem is high – suggesting that the self-enhancing effects of narcissism would be curtailed when the influence of narcissistic vulnerability, which is associated negatively with self-esteem is considered. Although narcissistic vulnerability did not account for the waning of narcissistic leader perceptions over time, it is possibly due to the explicit self-report assessment of what is considered an implicit construct of narcissism.

While it might seem that narcissistic vulnerability is a stumbling block towards narcissists achieving self-enhancement in the long-term, it could possibly act as a protective mechanism to safeguard narcissists' health and well-being. The beneficial health effects of narcissistic vulnerability are implied from the higher physiological stress narcissists experience in daily life, leading to the experience of negative emotions and in turn translating to higher cost to health and well-being. Thus, the high levels of stress experienced through the continuous pursuit of self-enhancement could be attenuated by targeting and achieving short-term self-enhancement that is activated by narcissistic vulnerability. Such a postulation, however, is speculative and warrants future research. Also warranting future research are other mechanisms and factors that underpin the modality of this proposed "time-bomb" mechanism.

The multidimensional nature of the NPI has also led to conceptualizations of adaptive and maladaptive narcissism. More specifically, the NPI's assessments of authority/leadership and self-sufficiency could be considered as adaptive, as they infer positive qualities such as assertiveness and self-confidence, while assessments of exploitativeness, exhibitionism and entitlement are considered maladaptive, as they seem to correspond to negative qualities such as hostility and impulsivity. From the perspective of narcissistic leadership temporality, it could be that narcissists' adaptive characteristics are more recognized relative to their maladaptive characteristics initially, leading to favorable perceptions of narcissists as leaders during leader emergence.

However, narcissistic leaders' adaptive characteristics might disappear and/or maladaptive characteristics might become more apparent over time, leading to the waning of favorable follower perceptions of narcissists as leaders over time. Future research can examine the concept of adaptive and maladaptive narcissism and whether it can contribute to the explanation for the temporal pattern of narcissists as leaders.

Narcissism, particularly narcissistic grandiosity, has been typically cast as agentic preservation of the self and found to be lacking in communal self-representations such as empathy and interpersonal warmth. The agency-communion model, however, posits that while the central focus of narcissism is to satisfy agentic self-motives, narcissists can achieve these agentic goals through communal means. This could mean that in leader-follower group dynamics, narcissistic leaders could engage in communal behaviors in order to achieve agentic outcomes. Thus, it is possible that favorable follower perceptions of narcissists as leaders initially are a consequence of narcissists' behaviors being judged as communal, even though these behaviors were agentically motivated. However, narcissistic leaders' continual engagement in communal behaviors over time might be hampered by their impulse to achieve agentic self-enhancement, thus leading to inconsistent and/or curtailed engagement in communal behaviors over time. Such a postulation offers a plausible explanation for the waning of follower perceptions of narcissistic leadership over time. Equally, it is possible that narcissistic leaders are judged as favorably as leaders for an extended period of time if they decide to utilize communal methods to achieving agentic self-enhancement. Such a prediction is plausible given narcissists' awareness of others' motives and emotions and their capacity to exhibit a range of communal behaviors like empathy that are contrary to mainstream characteristics of narcissism. A caveat of this prediction would be the presence of agentic outcomes that can be achieved over the long-term. If narcissists identify leader emergence as an agentic goal and not leader effectiveness, then it is unlikely that narcissists would persist with communal behaviors beyond the initial phase of leader emergence. Future research examining the temporal effects of communal narcissism on leadership across time could provide further understanding of how communal narcissism is associated with leadership across time, as well as the conditions that dictate the activation of communal narcissism in the context of leadership.

Narcissism and transformational leadership

Previous research examining the associations between narcissism and transformational leadership has been equivocal. The findings from this book suggest that these equivocal findings are most probably a consequence of the lack of consideration of temporality, since previous studies have largely been cross-sectional in design, and thus are only able to offer snapshots of perceptions towards narcissistic leadership.

The narcissists have the capacity to demonstrate appropriate transformational behaviors when they perceive that a certain context is self-enhancing (i.e., leader emergence), and not demonstrate transformational behaviors when they when a context is perceived as lacking in self-enhancement (i.e., leader effectiveness). If narcissists are aware of the transformational needs of followers and have the capacity to satisfy these needs, then as long as elements of self-enhancement are guaranteed in the long-term, narcissists could continue to be effective leaders. Regrettably, narcissistic self-enhancement outcomes are usually not neatly aligned with positive relationship outcomes, because narcissistic self-enhancement processes can sometimes lead to anti-social behaviors like aggression, self-handicapping and taking credit or blaming others. Such negative interpersonal outcomes are possibly a consequence of narcissists' inability to establish warm and emotionally intimate relationships, which further highlights narcissists' investment in extraverted and confident qualities when participating in social interactions as engaging in self-image preservation.

Given the focus of transformational leadership on the emotional aspect of the leader-follower relationship, the finding that transformational leadership explained the positive perceptions of narcissists as leaders initially but not, later on, suggests that it is the ability to emotionally connect with followers that are crucial for narcissistic leader-follower relationships to thrive. Perhaps the establishing of such emotional connections are only possible initially because of the bold, charismatic visions espoused by narcissistic leaders that are capable of rallying followers, but are also self-enhancing to narcissists as they attain leadership status; but not overtime as narcissistic leaders are found to be inactive in pursuing these socialized visions. If narcissistic leaders' lack of follow-through on their socialized visions is rectified, then the emotional connections between narcissistic leader and their followers can be maintained, which in turn increases the likelihood for narcissists to remain as effective leaders over time. Such a postulation is supported by recent research suggesting that narcissists are malleable towards more communal traits like empathy and humility, to the extent that it is possible for narcissists to self-enhance within a more communal paradigm by demonstrating more communal behavior. Thus, it would be interesting to examine if greater alignment of narcissistic self-enhancement goals with leader-follower relationship expectations can extend narcissistic leadership effectiveness across time.

The role of transformational leadership within the temporality of narcissistic leadership also gives rise to the debate on whether transformational leadership should be conceptualized and measured globally or differentially. There are different views in terms of which approach is best. The lack of clear theoretical distinctions and empirical distinctions between the transformational leadership components (i.e., the failure to confirm the factor structure of the proposed transformational leadership model and the strong intercorrelations between the components), seem to suggest a global approach to transformational leadership. Another advantage of taking a global approach is that it makes the process of data collection more straightforward, especially in complex experimental designs. Indeed, a global approach is recommended for initial explorations, which could be subsequently refined with a differentiated approach.

In contrast, following a differentiated approach would make possible the examination of the specific transformational leadership behaviours such as vision (i.e., inspirational motivation), support (i.e., individual consideration) and challenge (i.e., high performance expectations and intellectual stimulation) leadership behaviours and how they correspond to the different temporal phases of leadership and narcissistic traits.

When leader-follower relations are extended over time, characteristically "non-narcissistic" transformational leadership behaviors like challenge and support components could be increasingly sought after but are unlikely to be reciprocated by narcissistic leaders because they offer little in return in terms of self-enhancement. Furthermore, without the buffer of demonstrating the appropriate transformational leadership behaviors over time, self-enhancement intentions of the narcissistic leaders become more apparent and are likely to be negatively evaluated by followers, thus intensifying the waning of their perceptions towards narcissistic leaders over time. Future research can examine the independent explanatory effects of the differentiated components of transformational leadership on narcissistic leadership, to identify pertinence and propensity of certain components of transformational leadership behaviors at different points in time.

The temporality of narcissistic leadership is a product of evolution

In the same vein as evolutionary theorizing on social rank attainment, the dominance-prestige evolutionary account is a viable theoretical basis for explaining narcissistic leadership. The findings demonstrated that narcissists were perceived as both dominant and prestigious leaders during leader emergence, which is consistent with previous research suggesting dominance and prestige as two viable pathways to achieving leadership. Additionally, the distinctiveness of dominance and prestige approaches in achieving leadership suggests that narcissists are highly adaptive during leader emergence in achieving leadership. The findings immediately after leader emergence showed empirically the effectiveness of narcissists engaging in dominance strategies to maintain leadership status in a temporal phase that is prone to follower free-riding and ingroup bias as predicted in Service-for-Prestige. Nonetheless, whether narcissists have adapted to temporal demands of leadership immediately after leader emergence by taking a dominance approach or their preference for taking a dominance approach coincided well with the characteristics of the temporal phase immediately after leader emergence is unclear and warrants future research. Overall, taking a dominance-prestige account of narcissistic leadership temporality highlighted the unique leadership contexts that characterize specific temporal phases of leadership and the corresponding leadership characteristics that are required for leadership effectiveness.

The success of narcissists in achieving leader emergence by independently engaging in prestige and dominance strategies highlights the awareness and adaptability narcissists may possess when navigating through the complexities and uncertainties that are descriptive of leader emergent contexts. Narcissists seem to know instinctively that there exist two ways to the top and are comfortable in engaging in either strategy to maximize their chances of leadership under specific circumstances. The proposed emergence of narcissism as an evolved variant of dominance in a period when long-term cooperativeness was increasingly viable as a mating strategy, seems to support narcissists' dexterity when it comes to employing prestige or dominance strategies to achieve leader emergence. However, the lack of positive perceptions towards narcissistic leadership over the long-term suggests that narcissists are less evolved to succeed in leadership contexts in the long-term. Since narcissism has evolved from dominant mating strategies, it's default mode is likely to be that of dominance, which in turn implies their natural inclination to engage in dominance strategies – making any efforts to engage in prestige strategies increasingly challenging over time. Similarly, the idea of narcissism as an evolved trait characterized by explicit hubristic pride and implicit shame suggests that the weak basis of hubristic claims would be effective in the short-term (in its utility as a coping mechanism) but not in the long-term, especially when checked by feelings of shame. Such a notion is supported by the propensity for overconfident people to receive prestige and deference from others, which coincidentally provides an explanation for narcissists being perceived as both prestigious and dominant during leader emergence. Indeed, the social advantages in displaying overconfidence require individuals to engage in evolutionary self-deceptive self-enhancement – to convince themselves of their superior qualities before they can impress others with them. However, the cost of being overconfident is the possibility of not fulfilling previously communicated intentions over time, which is consistent with the evolutionary hubristic pride-shame account of narcissism, making it more difficult for narcissistic leaders to maintain their social standing as leaders. Thus, the evolutionary account of narcissistic leadership has provided new insights that explain its temporality and should be applied in future research.

Helping narcissistic leaders become more "temporally resilient"

There currently exist several proposals to help narcissists lead more effectively. The central idea behind these suggestions is the recognition of mutually beneficial outcomes for narcissists and their followers when narcissists emerge as leaders (i.e., narcissists are able to self-enhance while followers benefit in terms of group organization) and attempt to extend these mutual benefits over time. Instilling narcissistic leaders with "temporal resilience" requires the engagement in mutually beneficial strategies - enabling narcissists to constantly self-enhance when in leadership but in doing so, also allow followers to benefit from the actions of narcissistic leaders. Introducing regular leader performance goal appraisals could help to more accurately calibrate leadership goals to the effect it is challenging and sufficiently self-enhancing in regular short-term periods for narcissists, but also equally beneficial for followers. In order to manage narcissistic goal appraisals, organizations can either incorporate regular appraisals into the organization's formal staff review procedures or as proposed by Maccoby (2000), allow a trusted confidant/advisor who is rooted in reality to assist narcissistic leaders in their decision-making and goal-setting. These interventions can help to keep narcissistic self-enhancement in check – to ensure it is sufficiently self-enhancing for narcissists to be motivated to engage in positive leadership behaviors that would preserve and/or enhance their leadership effectiveness.

The finding that transformational leadership explained the perceptions of narcissistic leader effectiveness initially but not overtime seems to suggest that engaging in strategies to foster closer emotional bonds between narcissistic leaders and followers could also prove to be a worthwhile approach to increase narcissistic leader effectiveness over time. Indeed, transformational leadership has been described as making a link with followers by being generous, showing concern for followers, giving special attention to neglected others, treating followers as individuals and expressing appreciation when followers perform well (Bass, 1985). Bass (1985) also alluded to the empathic capabilities of transformational leaders that make them competent mentors, leading to suggestions that transformational (charismatic) leaders are sensitive to the needs of followers. Narcissists also seem to have an awareness of the benefits of engaging in close relationships with others or the detriments of not doing so. For example, narcissists are likely to realize that displaying narcissistic traits like superiority when working in groups would be counterproductive to their self-enhancement aims. Additionally, narcissists are highly adaptive in communal contexts in being able to successfully achieve self-enhancement through communal means. Furthermore, promising findings in the literature such as communal activation, sharing key similarities, humility, and perspective-taking could offer a basis for potential interventions that tap into the interpersonal connection between narcissistic leaders and followers to be implemented.

In the latter example, exposing narcissists to a perspective-taking paradigm led to higher empathic responses by narcissists, which suggests that previous observations of narcissists being low in empathy is automatic and can be elevated. Further, narcissists show an awareness of others' emotions (cognitive empathy) but lack in displaying the appropriate reactions in response to others' emotions. These findings imply that narcissists have the capacity and potential to be more empathic, and interventions like perspective-taking or empathy training can be implemented to induce narcissists to engage in more empathic behavior.

Another approach that can tap into both the charismatic/visionary strengths of narcissists and their potential to engage more synergistically with their followers is by encouraging narcissistic leaders to have higher organizational identification. Leader organizational identification refers to a leader's perceived "oneness" with the organization, where "the distinction between firm and self is minimized". When a leader is high in organizational identification, there is likely a greater congruence between the leader's and the organization's goals and performance outcomes. Increased goal congruence as a consequence of identifying more with the organization means that narcissistic leaders are more likely to demonstrate behaviors that are beneficial to the collective. Indeed, increasing goal congruence by designing individual goals to be more interdependent with other group members' goals has encouraged narcissistic leaders to engage in more team-oriented behavior that in turn led to better team performances.

However, narcissistic self-enhancement is still likely to persist even when narcissistic leaders are more highly identified with the organization; just that self-enhancement is less likely to be at the expense of the collective good.

With increased organizational identification, narcissistic leaders are also more likely to articulate socialized visions to achieve organizational success, and in doing so, followers would perceive narcissistic leaders as more charismatic/visionary. Articulating a socialized vision is linked to several positive outcomes for leaders which include gaining more acceptance from followers, more intent for followers to collaborate, share knowledge and make joint decisions, and higher levels of follower behavioral integration. Socialized visions articulated by narcissistic leaders are often bold and risky but yet are still accepted by followers as charismatic/visionary. Thus, the moderating effects of leader organizational identification on the relationship between narcissism and team behavioral integration and ultimately performance seem to imply that the negative effects of narcissistic leadership can be stemmed if leaders firmly align themselves to the organization. However, what is required (e.g., self-enhancement opportunities) to keep narcissistic leaders strongly identified with the organization over time, and whether leader organizational identification is effective over time in attenuating the negative effects of narcissistic leadership remain unclear and are areas worthy of future research. In essence, narcissistic leaders seem to have the capacity to engage in closer relationships with their followers, which leads to positive group outcomes; but whether forging closer relationships with followers can lead to a more "temporally resilient" brand of narcissistic leadership is still unclear and requires further empirical research.

Maccoby (2000) mooted the possibility of narcissistic leaders indoctrinating followers to submit to their ideologies as a way to maintain effective narcissistic leadership over time. Such a notion seems inconceivable; especially when in reality there usually exist exit strategies and alternatives available to followers. However, it is perhaps possible under conditions of a perceived threat from outgroups, for narcissistic leaders to achieve a degree of ideological submission from their followers. Known as collective narcissism, it is a concept of narcissism that extends into the interpersonal domain, where an ingroup is idealized instead of the self. The effects of ingroup bias according to Service-for-Prestige also support the probability of collective narcissism occurring under conditions of outgroup threat. However, whether the assumed coherence and homogeneity of ingroup greatness extend over the long-term is unknown. Given our conclusion that adopting a persistent dominance strategy is unlikely to extrapolate into effective narcissistic leadership over time, it seems that any positive effects of collective narcissism are unlikely to extend into the long-term. However, such a postulation remains speculative since the effects of collective narcissism have been observed across different social and cultural contexts and warrant future research.

Rethinking the leader selection process – leveling the narcissism bias

Another approach to addressing the destructive effects of narcissism in the long-term is to re-evaluate the processes of leader selection. Current leader selection and leader training processes seem to promote narcissistic characteristics that are favorable for leader emergence. Indeed, the interview method of leader selection could positively bias interviewer evaluations of more narcissistic candidates. An overemphasis on the qualities that encourage leader emergence would not only suit narcissists but also result in a higher concentration of narcissists in leadership positions.

Unsurprisingly, having more narcissists occupying leadership positions consequently leads to the temporality of narcissistic leadership being generalized as a universal phenomenon. More precisely, leadership in most contexts is likely to stagnate over time when there is overconfidence, homogeneity, and complacency, leading to what is termed as a "honeymoon effect" – a temporal pattern of leadership that is characterized by a familiar initial positive leadership that declines over time.

Since leader selection and recruitment processes favor the demonstration of narcissistic qualities, tertiary institutes of learning that are concerned with the employability of their students in an increasingly competitive job market, have started to equip students by training them to excel in current formats of leadership selection and recruitment and/or focus on short-term competitiveness. In a social climate where narcissism is reported to be steadily increasing, particularly amongst Generation Y, such educational foci on competing in the short-term only serve to reinforce the notion that narcissism is essential for a successful life.

Indeed, millennial students in business schools have been found to have high levels of narcissism, and expect greater success in securing employment, high salaries and promotions. It is telling that current mode of leader selection and recruitment, and by association leadership training in educational institutes are in need of updating, in order to shift some of the focus away from narcissism and instead examine other characteristics that are more predictive of temporally consistent leadership effectiveness. Incorporating other leader selection criteria not only makes recruitment more equitable, it also helps to identify more well-rounded candidates that are more suitable for leadership over the long-term. Furthermore, the changes in leader selection processes could reasonably result in ripple effects in education and more broadly on an entire generation, where narcissism is no longer seen as pivotal for success.

Conclusion

In conclusion, the findings from this book show empirically for the first time that the temporality of narcissistic leadership is characterized by initial positive follower perceptions that wane over time. This temporal pattern of narcissistic leadership can be explained by the perceptions of narcissists' ability to display transformational leadership behaviors for a short initial period. The explanatory effect of transformational leadership highlights the significance and also the fickleness of the emotional relationship between leader and followers in determining leadership effectiveness over time. Further insights into the temporality of narcissistic leadership were obtained from an evolutionary perspective; where the temporal pattern of narcissistic leadership is explained by distinct initial perceptions of narcissists as either dominant or prestigious individuals, as dominant individuals immediately after leader emergence, but not overtime. The findings, from an evolutionary perspective, suggest that narcissists are highly adaptable for the purposes of self-enhancement in the short-term, and therefore are very successful in leadership emergence contexts. However, we postulate that narcissists are likely to revert to their default evolutionary dominance strategies over time, which has shown to elicit positive perceptions of narcissists as leaders early on but not later. Investing in mutually beneficial strategies that focus on establishing closer relationships between narcissistic leaders and their followers, where narcissistic leaders are consistently motivated to self-enhance and their followers benefit from their leadership, is a promising approach to extending the positive effects of narcissistic leadership into the long-term. An alternative approach would be to rethink current leader selection and training processes to encourage a more broad-based appreciation of the different traits that are predictive of consistent, long-term leadership effectiveness. The relative benefit of each approach is likely context-specific.

Don't miss out!

Visit the website below and you can sign up to receive emails whenever Brittany Forrester publishes a new book. There's no charge and no obligation.

https://books2read.com/r/B-A-NLUP-SXGRB

BOOKS 2 READ

Connecting independent readers to independent writers.

Also by Brittany Forrester

Adult Survivors of Childhood Sexual Abuse The Effects On Mental Health And The Role Of Cognitive Behavior Therapy
Binge Killer The Use of Cognitive Behavioral Therapy to Address Shame in Binge Eating Disorder
Codependency Recovery Learn To Recognize Codependent Traits And Overcome Them
A Guide for the Psychosocial Treatment of Infertility
Emdr Toolbox A Powerful StrategyOf Self Through Eye Movement Desensitization and Reprocessing Therapy
Emotional Sugar Understanding Sugar Addiction, Through the Lens of Emotional Regulation
Face Failure Characteristics of Leaders Who Have Successfully Recovered from Significant Setbacks
Narcissism And Leadership
Childhood Experiences of Sibling Abuse An Investigation into Learned Helplessness
End Panic Attacks And Stop Anxiety
Self-Regulation Skills How To Control And Regulate The Learning Process
The Self-Esteem Workbook The multiple forms of self-esteem and the evaluation of one's value
The Shame Complex A Depth Psychological Exploration of Shame
Brain Healing and Trauma How Dark Psychology is Highly Effective in Treating Adult Survivors of Childhood Abuse

Complex Ptsd Recovery Understanding and treating Complex Trauma Using Emdr and Concepts from Individual Psychology
Defiant Children When Your Kid isn't Just Difficult
The Ultimate Diabetes Cookbook Take Control of your Type 2 Diabetes with a Complete Meal plan and Tons of Delicious Recipes
A Complete Guide to Parent Attachment How to Help Children to Heal From Trauma and Learn the Skills They Need for Successful Relationships

Ingram Content Group UK Ltd.
Milton Keynes UK
UKHW020834210723
425555UK00014B/536

9 798201 441425